ACKNOWLEDGMENTS

Independent Bookstore Day would like to thank all
the poets and publishers who generously donated
the work herein to benefit indie bookstores and
the book-loving public.

POEMS OF RESISTANCE POEMS OF HOPE

WITH POEMS BY JOY HARJO, ADA LIMÓN, HANIF ABDURRAQIB, MORGAN PARKER AND MANY MORE CONTEMPORARY POETS

A $6 STORY

TABLE OF CONTENTS

LET THEM NOT SAY

JANE HIRSHFIELD

Let them not say: we did not see it.
We saw.

Let them not say: we did not hear it.
We heard.

Let them not say: they did not taste it.
We ate, we trembled.

Let them not say: it was not spoken, not written.
We spoke,
we witnessed with voices and hands.

Let them not say: they did nothing.
We did not-enough.

Let them say, as they must say something:

A kerosene beauty.
It burned.

Let them say we warmed ourselves by it,
read by its light, praised,
and it burned.

THE LEASH

ADA LIMÓN

After the birthing of bombs of forks and fear,
the frantic automatic weapons unleashed,
the spray of bullets into a crowd holding hands,
that brute sky opening in a slate-metal maw
that swallows only the unsayable in each of us, what's
left? Even the hidden nowhere river is poisoned
orange and acidic by a coal mine. How can
you not fear humanity, want to lick the creek
bottom dry, to suck the deadly water up into
your own lungs, like venom? Reader, I want to
say: *Don't die*. Even when silvery fish after fish
comes back belly up, and the country plummets
into a crepitating crater of hatred, isn't there still
something singing? The truth is: I don't know.
But sometimes, I swear I hear it, the wound closing
like a rusted-over garage door, and I can still move
my living limbs into the world without too much
pain, can still marvel at how the dog runs straight
toward the pickup trucks break-necking down
the road, because she thinks she loves them,
because she's sure, without a doubt, that the loud
roaring things will love her back, her soft small self

alive with desire to share her goddamn enthusiasm,
until I yank the leash back to save her because
I want her to survive forever. *Don't die,* I say,
and we decide to walk for a bit longer, starlings
high and fevered above us, winter coming to lay
her cold corpse down upon this little plot of earth.
Perhaps we are always hurtling our body towards
the thing that will obliterate us, begging for love
from the speeding passage of time, and so maybe,
like the dog obedient at my heels, we can walk together
peacefully, at least until the next truck comes.

DUPLEX

JERICHO BROWN

I begin with love, hoping to end there.
I don't want to leave a messy corpse.

    I don't want to leave a messy corpse
    Full of medicines that turn in the sun.

Some of my medicines turn in the sun.
Some of us don't need hell to be good.

    Those who need most, need hell to be good.
    What are the symptoms of your sickness?

Here is one symptom of my sickness:
Men who love me are men who miss me.

    Men who leave me are men who miss me
    In the dream where I am an island.

In the dream where I am an island,
I grow green with hope. I'd like to end there.

BRUTE STRENGTH

EMILY SKAJA

Soldier for a lost cause, brute, mute woman
written out of my own story, I've been trying
to cast a searchlight over swamp-woods & parasitic ash
back to my beginning, that girlhood—
kite-wisp clouded by gun salutes & blackbirds
tearing out from under the hickories
all those fine August mornings so temporary
so gold-ringed by heat haze & where is that witch girl
unafraid of anything, flea-spangled little yard rat, runt
of no litter, queen, girl who wouldn't let a boy hit her,
girl refusing to be It in tag, pulling that fox hide
heavy around her like a flag? Let me look at her.
Tell her on my honor, I will set the wedding dress on fire
when I'm good & ready or she can bury me in it.

WHAT IS TRAGEDY?
ALISON C. ROLLINS

Inside everything I have ever written
there is a girl—strange and alive.
Her sex is formed one image at a time:
pistachio shells in trash can, an animal
pretending to be dead, a fur-covered
moth, taffeta arranged in velvet clumps.
I know not what this world will do to
her or how her mother will someday
find her body. She sees white before
she blacks out, the texture of her
tongue like silt. If I slept with the girl
what would *sleep* imply? I stroke her hair.
Almost like a mother. I smell her as she
dreams of cottonwoods and caterpillars.
The light shifts and I am left childless
staring at the shape of fog. Someday,
when I am gone, this will all make sense,
how the girl held my poems like fetishes
in her mouth, sucked on words: *welt, sift,
cleave,* and *burr,* how poetic she was when full,
waiting quietly for terror to find her.

CONTOURING THE FLATTENING

CAMONGHNE FELIX

I try not to tell about the stories
still bleeding. After all, who wishes
to lead their own mother to wolves.

I try not to mess with the shape of
my privilege. I only say what they
need to hear. If the they is an us
I make myself an example. I lie to
keep it all intact.

But if I felt I could, I would unstitch
this plaque sewn over my
mouth. I would tell you of the seasonal

allergies, how my primary doctor warned
my mother of dead cockroaches, their
eggs, the likelihood of them in my lungs.

I would tell of how often we'd bomb the house,
how I'd spend summer nights collecting little brown
skeletons in the thousands, every inhale ending
in a question of poison.

I would tell of the mice that sometimes bit
us in our sleep, how the infestation of them
violated any concept of domain—how
we could not know who the house really
belonged to; a house of rodents, or of men

but I keep my sob stories to myself.[1] I keep my
smile white and fists closed. I let survival be
survival. I grow into the shoe. I keep the world
big and my sanity small.

[1] *I was almost killed in that water and I've had a fear ever since*

HEAVY

HIEU MINH NGUYEN

The narrow clearing down to the river
I walk alone, out of breath

my body catching on each branch.
Small children maneuver around me.

Often, I want to return to my old body
a body I also hated, but hate less

given knowledge.
Sometimes my friends—my friends

who are always beautiful & heartbroken
look at me like they know

I will die before them.
I think the life I want

is the life I have, but how can I be sure?
There are days when I give up on my body

but not the world.
I am alive. I know this. Alive now

to see the world, to see the river
rupture everything with its light.

THEORY OF MEMORY

LOUISE GLÜCK

Long, long ago, before I was a tormented artist, afflicted with longing yet incapable of forming durable attachments, long before this, I was a glorious ruler uniting all of a divided country—so I was told by the fortune-teller who examined my palm. Great things, she said, are ahead of you, or perhaps behind you; it is difficult to be sure. And yet, she added, what is the difference? Right now you are a child holding hands with a fortune-teller. All the rest is hypothesis and dream.

IT WAS SUMMER NOW AND THE COLORED PEOPLE CAME OUT INTO THE SUNSHINE

MORGAN PARKER

They descend from the boat two by two. The gap in
Angela Davis's teeth speaks to the gap in James Baldwin's
teeth. The gap in James Baldwin's teeth speaks to the
gap in Malcom X's teeth. The gap in Malcom X's teeth
speaks to the gap in Malcom X's teeth. The gap in
Condoleezza Rice's teeth doesn't speak. Martin Luther
King Jr. Boulevard kisses the Band-Aid on Nelly's cheek.
Frederick Douglass's side part kisses Nikki Giovanni's
"Thug Life" tattoo. The choir is led by Whoopi Goldberg's
eyebrows. The choir is led by Will Smith's flat top.
The choir loses its way. The choir never returns home.
The choir sings funeral instead of wedding, sings funeral
instead of allegedly, sings funeral instead of help, sings
Black instead of grace, sings Black as knucklebone,
mercy, junebug, sea air. It is time for war.

CHAPTER III

CHASE BERGGRUN

Let me begin with observation

My concern is with agency

I was satisfied with my body

My desire is my own

my smile   my own

I unsealed the seriousness of sound

Freedom melted in the weatherworn abyss

Some weird effect of shadow

could allow an opportunity to resist

I took pleasure   in disobeying

I determined not to compose myself

I suppose I was not unchanged

I thought I felt desire kiss me with red lips

Never could I be a girl on her knees

I was a storm of a woman

transformed with red light

heaving an imperious voice

forward into the dimness

BLACK MATTERS

KEITH S. WILSON

after D.H. Lawrence

shall i tell you, then, that we exist?
there came a light, blue and white careening,
the police like wailing angels
to bitter me.

and so this:
dark matter is hypothetical. know
that it cannot be seen

in the gunpowder of a flower,
in a worm that raisins on the concrete,
in a man that wills himself not to speak.

gags, oh gags.
for a shadow cannot breathe.
it deprives them of nothing. pride

is born in the black and dies in it.
i hear our shadow, low treble
of the clasping of our hands.

dark matter is invisible.
we infer it: how light bends around a black body,
and still you do not see black halos, even here,

my having told you plainly where they are.

AMERICAN ARITHMETIC

NATALIE DIAZ

Native Americans make up less than
one percent of the population of America.
0.8 percent of 100 percent.

O, mine efficient country.

I do not remember the days before America—
I do not remember the days when we were all here.

Police kill Native Americans more
than any other race. *Race* is a funny word.
Race implies someone will win,
implies *I have as good a chance of winning as*—

Who wins the race that isn't a race?

Native Americans make up 1.9 percent of all
police killings, higher per capita than any race—

Sometimes *race* means *run*.

I'm not good at math—can you blame me?
I've had an American education.

We are Americans, and we are less than 1 percent
of Americans. We do a better job of dying
by police than we do existing.

When we are dying, who should we call?
The police? Or our senator?
Please, someone, call my mother.

At the National Museum of the American Indian,
68 percent of the collection is from the United States.
I am doing my best to not become a museum
of myself. I am doing my best to breathe in and out.
I am begging: *Let me be lonely but not invisible.*

But in an American room of one hundred people,
I am Native American—less than one, less than
whole—I am less than myself. Only a fraction
of a body, let's say, *I am only a hand*—

and when I slip it beneath the shirt of my lover
I disappear completely.

WE LIVED HAPPILY DURING THE WAR

ILYA KAMINSKY

And when they bombed other people's houses, we

protested
but not enough, we opposed them but not

enough. I was
in my bed, around my bed America

was falling: invisible house by invisible house by invisible
house.

I took a chair outside and watched the sun.

In the sixth month
of a disastrous reign in the house of money

in the street of money in the city of money in the country
of money,
our great country of money, we (forgive us)

lived happily during the war.

IF THEY SHOULD COME FOR US

FATIMAH ASGHAR

these are my people & I find
them on the street & shadow
through any wild all wild
my people my people
a dance of strangers in my blood
the old woman's sari dissolving to wind
bindi a new moon on her forehead
I claim her my kin & sew
the star of her to my breast
the toddler dangling from stroller
hair a fountain of dandelion seed
at the bakery I claim them too
the sikh uncle at the airport
who apologizes for the pat
down the muslim man who abandons
his car at the traffic light drops
to his knees at the call of the azan
& the muslim man who sips
good whiskey at the start of maghrib
the lone khala at the park
pairing her kurta with crocs
my people my people I can't be lost

when I see you my compass
is brown & gold & blood
my compass a muslim teenager
snapback & high-tops gracing
the subway platform
mashallah I claim them all
my country is made
in my people's image
if they come for you they
come for me too in the dead
of winter a flock of
aunties steps out on the sand
their dupattas turn to ocean
a colony of uncles grind their palms
& a thousand jasmines bell the air
my people I follow you like constellations
we hear the glass smashing the street
& the nights opening their dark
our names this country's wood
for the fire my people my people
the long years we've survived the long
years yet to come I see you map
my sky the light your lantern long
ahead & I follow I follow

MASS FOR PENTECOST: CANTICLE FOR BIRDS & WATERS

D.A. POWELL

There is no cause to grieve among the living or the dead,
       so long as there is music in the air.

And where the water and the air divide, I'll take you there.
       The levee aureate with yellow thistles.
White moth, wasp and dragonfly.
             We could not wish unless it were on wings.
Give us our means and point us toward the sun.

Will the spirit come to us now in the pewter paten of the air,
       the fluted call of dabbler drakes, the deadpan honk
            of the white-fronted goose, the tule goose.
Tongues confused in the matchstick rushes.
       High, high the baldpate cries, and in the air,
and in the air, the red-winged blackbirds chase the damselflies.

Triumph over death with me. And we'll divide the air.

OLIVE HARVEST

FRED MARCHANT

It's true, the tree has the scent of the sea,
but the silver leaves, their slender fingers,

the thick, infinitely twined trunk, some riddle
in the roots that lets it drink from the stones,

even the place where a limb has broken or
been lopped off, the shoot that springs back

to life, stumps that burn for hour upon hour,
a scattered discard twig you press to your lips,

and the fruit that hangs from young branches
and old, a green reddening to black, this fruit

ripened on enough bloodshed and hardened
human behavior to make you think it will turn

away in disgust, year after suffering year
comes back, as if to say *here & here & here*

BULLET POINTS

JERICHO BROWN

I will not shoot myself
In the head, and I will not shoot myself
In the back, and I will not hang myself
With a trash bag, and if I do,
I promise you, I will not do it
In a police car while handcuffed
Or in the jail cell of a town
I only know the name of
Because I have to drive through it
To get home. Yes, I may be at risk,
But I promise you, I trust the maggots
And the ants and the roaches
Who live beneath the floorboards
Of my house to do what they must
To any carcass more than I trust
An officer of the law of the land
To shut my eyes like a man
Of God might, or to cover me with a sheet
So clean my mother could have used it
To tuck me in. When I kill me, I will
Do it the same way most Americans do,
I promise you: cigarette smoke

Or a piece of meat on which I choke
Or so broke I freeze
In one of these winters we keep
Calling worst. I promise if you hear
Of me dead anywhere near
A cop, then that cop killed me. He took
Me from us and left my body, which is,
No matter what we've been taught,
Greater than the settlement
A city can pay a mother to stop crying,
And more beautiful than the new bullet
Fished from the folds of my brain.

ENLIGHTENED DESPOTISM

ARIANA REINES

It must be the full
Moon making me
So round she wrote
Predictably. Less
Room under that
Sweatshirt there.
Bra cutting into
The back. You
Look very pretty
Today Miss says
A man outside
The deli. Adulthood.
As though she
Were somebody's
Mother. Or it
Was more conceptual
Than that: the idea
Of motherhood was
All a softening body
Would now swallow
& arrange itself around
Was she to remain
Afraid of pleasure, sugar

Bread, fucking, forgetting
The struggle, forgetting
The real drama at hand
Body and face built
To prevaricate forever
In the enlightened
Despotism of some
Mind you could replenish
at will via PayPal

AMUSE-BOUCHE

MAX RITVO (1990-2016)

It is rare that I
have to stop eating anything
because I have run out of it.

We, in the West, eat until we want
to eat something else,
or want to stop eating altogether.

The chef of a great kitchen
uses only small plates.

He puts a small plate in front of me,
knowing I will hunger on for it
even as the next plate is being
placed in front of me.

But each plate obliterates the last
until I no longer mourn the destroyed plate,

but only mewl for the next,
my voice flat with comfort and faith.

And the chef is God,
whose faithful want only the destruction
of His prior miracles to make way
for new ones.

THE WINGS OF THE HASTILY ASSEMBLED ANGEL

SHANE MCCRAE

The hastily assembled angel flies

With patchwork wings red patches and white patches

And yellow patches blood and emptiness

And sun and usually   an angel's wings would

Be made of only one of these   but his

Were made at the last minute and were almost

Not made at all and wouldn't have been made

Had Azrael not seen   in the hastily

Assembled angel's eyes as Azrael

Placed his white palm on the hastily assembled

Angel's chest fear   as Azrael placed his palm there

To shove him from the cloud   and saw he had

No wings   and paused and thought   then pulled him back

And so the angels stitched together what was

Near   blood   emptiness   sun   as what was near

Was Heaven   and what else would Heaven be

HOW CAN BLACK PEOPLE WRITE ABOUT FLOWERS AT A TIME LIKE THIS

HANIF ABDURRAQIB

i maybe should have mentioned before this cruel unfurling began:
i only believe in god so that i might have someone else to task
with the blistered fingers & the trench of guilt they are responsible for
placing in the direct center of any room where you desire
a shrinking of the distance between us. but it has been said
that the first carnation bloomed from a tear of the virgin
mary which fell while jesus carried the cross with blood
streaming into his eyes. this is the part about a mother's
love. how i wore a carnation at the tip of a suit jacket on a night
a mother fought back tears & begged me to not do her daughter
wrong. & so here, let's make a deal. bring to me your palms
overflowing with the production of your most intemperate
anguish & i promise there is no target i will not stand in front of
for you. there is no wood that could fashion a cross to hold me.

TO EVERY FAGGOT WHO PULVERIZED ME FOR BEING A FAGGOT

JUSTIN PHILLIP REED

You were right to tell yourself
you'd never live this. You wouldn't
have survived. Each time my carpal flex
flashed open and stained whatever
clean appliance—rim of tub, my own
teeth where I sucked the wound quiet—
with its rouge run-off, I watched you
run off. I've told that story. I've taken a look
at the slow sea monster of my vomit
luminous in the toilet bowl, two digits
of my fingers still slick, nearly
erotic with gag slime: there was
my cocktail of daily medicine, half
digested. There was a line of folk
ready to tell me Black men don't do this
to themselves. They don't, you said,
take dick either, but here I am. There
you are. Some night I was so hungry and tired
and high on my prescription, I let
a man I didn't know feed me vodka

and orange juice until I would remember
neither my dreams nor his hands.
In three of the five psych wards I nested in
like a nomad bird—because where else
could I rest—I fell in love easily. I once stepped
entirely into a bottle of pills and tried to screw
my body finally underground. My father
lifted me seizing into a hospital and out
of his house shortly thereafter. Dear fellow
gay-ass nigga, who loves you these days?
I hope it's Black people. I hope no one
stole the certainty of that away from you.
To believe that white men had my back
was a facile act: who else so long
prepared to help me hate me?
I've told this story. I barely graduated.
I stunted my own growth. I don't know how
to go home. What you don't know is
I needed someone like you but braver. Now
I just have issues with needing anyone at all.
Your wife is shrugging out of a nightgown
and sinking under sheets. There are
drippings of me still between
your teeth. You've since taken
men in your mouth and said a silent
word to God. You could lie
there beside her wholly without conflict

or bitterness. She could be he. They
could be happy and the world
in which I've learned I live no less itself.
From its stubborn clay I've shaped
a creature, hollowed into its guts
a pair of lungs, attached appendages
that make it capable of walking
out of every room it enters at will
and willed it to love. What have you done.

DEAR BROTHER

JAKE SKEETS

You kissed a man the way I do

                            but with a handgun. You called it; I'm the fag

we were afraid to know, the one we'd throw rocks at, huff at like horses.

I learned to touch a man by touching myself. I learned to be a man by loving one.

Prison is not the chicken wire we'd get tangled in. Remember our bloodied

knees and bloody palms from mangled handlebars, beer bottles,

       and cactus spines? Remember the horned toad

                        we didn't mean to kill?

Our silence—thick as the dust kicked up by our skinny legs. You are still

that silence. Still that boy holding a deflated body

                        with your dawning hands.

EPITHALAMION

FADY JOUDAH

We hold the present responsible for my hand
in your hand, my thumb

as aspirin leaves a painless bruise, our youth
immemorial in a wormhole for silence

to rescue us, the heart free at last
of the tongue (the dream, the road) upon

which our hours reside together alone,
that this is love's profession, our scents

on pillows displace our alphabet to grass
with fidelity around our wrists

and breastbones, thistle and heather.
And this steady light, angular

through the window, is no amulet
to store in a dog-eared book.

A body exits all pages to be
inscribed on another, itself.

THE BOOK IS THE HOUSE

ELENI SIKELIANOS

THE BOOK IS THE HOUSE where the bodies are buried
the book is the catacombs where the corpses enumerate
the book is the joy is the place where the copses unfold happy, fragrant, & shining
the book is the meat sliding inside the bear and the bear inside its blanketing fur
the book is the joy was lost on the horizon
as hours flooded in
the trees kissed across the distances, & the sun
mirrored
in its pages the lake
therefore lung-ed as any animal I leaf
the wide pages flammable with life

AN OLD STORY

TRACY K. SMITH

We were made to understand it would be
Terrible. Every small want, every niggling urge,
Every hate swollen to a kind of epic wind.

Livid, the land, and ravaged, like a rageful
Dream. The worst in us having taken over
And broken the rest utterly down.

A long age

Passed. When at last we knew how little
Would survive us—how little we had mended

Or built that was not now lost—something
Large and old awoke. And then our singing
Brought on a different manner of weather.

Then animals long believed gone crept down
From trees. We took new stock of one another.
We wept to be reminded of such color.

MUSLIM GIRL PREAMBLE

RUMSHA SAJID

We the sisters of every color
in order to form a more perfect union
establish the sanctity
of elbows touching between women
while standing in prayer.
We preserve justice
through tucking our
homegirl's stray hair
back into her hijab when
she doesn't notice her ponytail is out.
During Ramadan
when our periods sync up
we will go
out for lunch together.
By the powers vested in us
we will not be called
last to eat at the fam jam
or let you expect us
to babysit aunties' kids at the mosque.
We secure our sisterhood
by knowing there is enough
baraqah for us all

therein never comparing our noor
with another sister's.
We solemnly swear to never silence
ourselves for your comfort
and support each other's journey
to peace from
this dunya to
the akhira.
Insha'Allah.

LOVE POEM

JON SANDS

Can I hand you my backpack and get loose?
My toe needs to sketch a snake on the sidewalk.
You don't mind if I shimmy and talk, yeah?
Is that a basketball? Let me trade you
these tax forms for it. I know this is an odd way
to propose, but I'm just gonna dance near you.
Soon, I won't even need to write poems.
You'll just look at my face and think,
That shit was deep. I'll twinkle an eyebrow;
you'll see my grandfather alone at the kitchen table
with the game on in the living room.
Or, I'll roll up my sleeve and you'll say,
You want to drink all my what?
I'll say, That was supposed to be
a heart metaphor, but I'm working on it!
Let me play you a song you'll like,
not just one I can prove I know all the words to.
I know we both love a different you,
but that's just how I do polyamory.
I have a spell for this, it's called Time-Machine.
That's Latin for I-wish-this-had-gone-differently.

Did you just turn my arm into a pterodactyl?
Is that an amoeba in your handbag?
Did the world just flip back to song one?
I wrote this for you, it's called The Bible:
just some shit I've been thinking about.
Let's create everything else. You know
what these ancient Egyptians need? Drake.
Poof, I just invented strawberries and syrup
then manifested myself love handles.
Oh, this old thing? I call that music.
Let's dance.

GHAZAL, AFTER FERGUSON

YUSEF KOMUNYAKAA

Somebody go & ask Biggie to orate
what's going down in the streets.

No, an attitude is not a suicide note
written on walls around the streets.

Twitter stays lockstep in the frontal lobe
as we hope for a bypass beyond the streets,

but only each day bears witness
in the echo chamber of the streets.

Grandmaster Flash's thunderclap says
he's not the grand jury in the streets,

says he doesn't care if you're big or small
fear can kill a man on the streets.

Take back the night. Take killjoy's
cameras & microphones to the streets.

If you're holding the hand lightning strikes
juice will light you up miles from the streets

where an electric chair surge dims
all the county lights beyond the streets.

Who will go out there & speak laws
of motion & relativity in the streets?

Yusef, this morning proves a crow
the only truth serum in the street.

(CITIZEN) (ILLEGAL)

JOSÉ OLIVAREZ

Mexican woman (illegal) and Mexican man (illegal) have
a Mexican (illegal)-American (citizen).
Is the baby more Mexican or American?
Place the baby in the arms of the mother (illegal).
If the mother holds the baby (citizen)
too long, does the baby become illegal?

The baby is a boy (citizen). He goes to school (citizen).
His classmates are American (citizen). He is outcast (illegal).
His "Hellos" are in the wrong language (illegal).
He takes the hyphen separating loneliness (Mexican)
from friendship (American) and jabs it at the culprit (illegal).
Himself (illegal). His own traitorous tongue (illegal).
His name (illegal). His mom (illegal). His dad (illegal).

Take a Mexican woman (illegal) and a Mexican man (illegal).
If they have a baby and the baby looks white enough to pass (citizen).
If the baby grows up singing Selena songs to his reflection (illegal).
If the baby hides from el cucuy and la migra (illegal).
If the baby (illegal) (citizen) grows up to speak broken Spanish (illegal)
and perfect English (citizen). If the boy's nickname is Güerito (citizen).
If the boy attends college (citizen). If the boy only dates women (illegal)
of color (illegal). If the boy (illegal) uses phrases like Women of Color (citizen).

If the boy (illegal) (citizen) writes (illegal) poems (illegal).
If the boy (citizen) (illegal) grows up (illegal) and can only write (illegal)
this story in English (citizen), does that make him more
American (citizen) or Mexican (illegal)?

AN AMERICAN SUNRISE

JOY HARJO

We were running out of breath, as we ran out to meet ourselves, We
Were surfacing the edge of our ancestors' fights, and ready to Strike
It was difficult to lose days in the Indian bar if you were Straight.
Easy if you played pool and drank to remember to forget. We
Made plans to be professional—and did. And some of us could Sing
When we drove to the edge of the mountains, with a drum. We
Made sense of our beautiful crazed lives under the starry stars. Sin
Was invented by the Christians, as was the Devil, we sang. We
Were the heathens, but needed to be saved from them: Thin
Chance. We knew we were all related in this story, a little Gin
Will clarify the dark, and make us all feel like dancing. We
Had something to do with the origins of blues and jazz
I argued with the music as I filled the jukebox with dimes in June,

Forty years later and we still want justice. We are still America. We.

BUEN ESQUELETO

NATALIE SCENTERS-ZAPICO

Life is short & I tell this to mis hijas.
Life is short & I show them how to talk
to police without opening the door, how
to leave the Social Security number blank
on the exam, I tell this to mis hijas.
This world tells them I hate you every day
& I don't keep this from mis hijas
because of the bus driver who kicks them out
onto the street for fare evasion. Because I love
mis hijas, I keep them from men who'd knock
their heads together just to hear the chime.
Life is short & the world is terrible. I know
no kind strangers in this country who aren't
sisters a desert away & I don't keep this
from mis hijas. It's not my job to sell
them the world, but to keep them safe
in case I get deported. Our first
landlord said with a bucket of bleach
the mold would come right off. He shook
mis hijas, said they had good bones
for hard work. Mi'jas, could we make this place
beautiful? I tried to make this place beautiful.

EPISTLE

JENNY XIE

Eavesdropping on a mother
needling at her mule-brained son
stopping by the side of the road
to examine the dry socket of Agios Georgios
the root of this self-denial is long
all those years I was spared of seeing myself through myself
Now the stifling days disrobe
distance giving autonomy the arid space to grow
I'll rinse later this afternoon in the sea
then compose lines to you of reasonable length
to say the opening you left is wide enough for me
but I'm stunned to love aloneness

DIAGNOSIS

KATHY FAGAN

I wasn't made to live alone. One
night there's a sky with clouds by Magritte,
the next I'm headed over the guardrail,
and who do I tell? My Ideal Reader?
Choices narrow as we age,
like my spine in the nave of its body.
I grew hollow waiting for your face,
like a drum beneath a hand that never
opens. To say sail is too nautical,
to say soufflé—well, then I forget
what I'm talking about...

      The ocean stayed still.
And the cows stayed on the hills
between us.

      I don't know if my spine will
ever close its trefoil window. I don't know
if I will never see you again. It is inferred
or it is infrared. Either way, my leaves fell.
And it took a good while, but I grew new
ones. Then the birds came back.

EVERGREEN

OLIVER BAEZ BENDORF

What still grows in winter?
Fingernails of witches and femmes,
green moss on river rocks
lit with secrets. I let myself
go near the river but not
the railroad: this is my bargain.
Water boils in a kettle in the woods
and I can hear the train grow louder
but I also can't, you know?
Then I'm shaving in front of an
unbreakable mirror while a nurse
watches over my shoulder.
Damn. What still grows in winter?
Lynda brought me basil I crushed
with my finger and thumb just to
smell the inside. So I go
to the river but not the rail-
road, think I'll live another year.
River rock digs into my shoulders
like a lover who knows I don't want
power. I release every muscle against
the rock, give it all my warmth.

Snow shakes
onto my chest quick as table salt.
Branches above me full of pine needles
whip: when the river rock is done
with me, I could belong to the evergreen.
Safety is a rock I throw into the river.
My body is ready. I don't even think
a train runs through this town anymore.

HIVE

KEVIN YOUNG

The honey bees' exile
    is almost complete.
You can carry

them from hive
    to hive, the child thought
& that is what

he tried, walking
    with them thronging
between his pressed palms.

Let him be right.
    Let the gods look away
as always. Let this boy

who carries the entire
    actual, whirring
world in his calm

unwashed hands,
    barely walking, bear
us all there

buzzing, unstung.

LEAVING THE PAIN CLINIC

WILLIAM BREWER

Always this warm moment when I forget which part of me
I blamed. Never mind the pills kicking in, their spell
that showers the waiting room, once full of shame,
in a soft rain of sparks that pity sometimes is,
how it mends the past like a welder seams metal,
and isn't that why we're all here, addicts
and arthritics—we close our eyes completely
but the edges only blur—and though the door's the same,
somehow the exit, like the worst wounds, is greater
than the entrance was. I throw it open for all to see
how daylight, so tall, has imagination. It has heart. It loves.

THE STRONG BY THEIR STILLNESS

CARL PHILLIPS

Most mornings here, mist is the first thing to go—first
the mist, then the fog, though hardly anyone seems to know
the difference, or even care, the way for some a dead buck
is a dead buck: the road, the body, a little light, the usual
dark, light's

                unshakeable escort...You can love a man
more than he'll ever love back or be able to, you can confuse
your understanding of that

                        with a thing like acceptance or,
worse, all you've ever deserved. I've driven hard into
the gorgeousness of spring before; it fell hard behind me:
the turning away, I mean, the finding of clothes,
the maneuvering

                awkwardly back into them...why not drive
forever? Respect or shame, it's pretty much your
own choice, is how it once got explained to me. I've already
said—I'm not sorry. Magnolia. Wild pear. So what if one
wish begets a next one,

                only to be conquered by it, if the blooms
break open nevertheless like hope?

WAR RUG

HENRI COLE

The pony and the deer are trapped by tanks,
and the lady with the guitar is sad beyond words.
Hurtling across the sky, a missile has mistaken
a vehicle for a helicopter, exploding in a ball
of white flame. Upside-down birds—red specks
of knotted wool—glow above the sideways trees.
Hidden among plants, a barefooted boy waits—
like the divine coroner—aiming his rifle at something,
enjoying the attentions of a gray doggy, or maybe
there's a bullet already in his head.

MONOLITH

YUSEF KOMUNYAKAA

The faces of Pussy Riot
move through the crowd
on a placard in Kiev, mist
of breath & weather rising,
& then tear gas & bullets.

A chorus of protestors fall
dead in snow, the woman
still holding to her sign.
Okay, friend, we can talk
about Victor Hugo,

how tomorrow hides inside
yesterday, how an emperor
marked his name on air
as half-dead soldiers hid
in the bellies of horses.

But let's come back to vigils
burned out & flowers heaped
around Independence Square,
to the after-sound of rock bands
in the night's cold epitaph.

FOR KEEPS

JOY HARJO

Sun makes the day new.
Tiny green plants emerge from earth.
Birds are singing the sky into place.
There is nowhere else I want to be but here.
I lean into the rhythm of your heart to see where it will
    take us.
We gallop into a warm, southern wind.
I link my legs to yours and we ride together,
Toward the ancient encampment of our relatives.
Where have you been? they ask.
And what has taken you so long?
That night after eating, singing, and dancing
We lay together under the stars.
We know ourselves to be part of mystery.
It is unspeakable.
It is everlasting.
It is for keeps.

March 4, 2013, Champaign, Illinois

ODE TO DIRT

SHARON OLDS

Dear dirt, I am sorry I slighted you,
I thought that you were only the background
for the leading characters—the plants
and animals and human animals.
It's as if I had loved only the stars
and not the sky which gave them space
in which to shine. Subtle, various,
sensitive, you are the skin of our terrain,
you're our democracy. When I understood
I had never honored you as a living
equal, I was ashamed of myself,
as if I had not recognized
a character who looked so different from me,
but now I can see us all, made of the
same basic materials—
cousins of that first exploding from nothing—
in our intricate equation together. O dirt,
help us find ways to serve your life,
you who have brought us forth, and fed us,
and who at the end will take us in
and rotate with us, and wobble, and orbit.

ANTHRACITE

SAEED JONES

A voice mistook for stone,
jagged black fist

thrown miles through space, through
doors of dark matter.

Heard you crack open the field's skull
where you landed.

Halo of smoke ruined the sky
and you were a body now

naked and bruised in the cratered cotton.
Could have been a meteorite

except for those strip-mined eyes, each
a point of fossilized night.

Bringing water and a blanket,
I asked, "Which of your lives is this,

third or fifth?" Your answer, blues
a breeze to soak my clothes

in tears. With my palm pressed
to your lips, hush. When they hear

you, they will want you. Beware
of how they want you;

in this town everything born black
also burns.

SHEA BUTTER MANIFESTO

EVE L. EWING

We, the forgotten delta people.
The dry riverbed people,
Hair calling always for rain,
Skin turned skyward wishing for clouds,
We stand for blood.
We kneel for water.
For oil, we lay down,
Fingers spread, as if in this way
we might skate across the yellow clay of it all
Like lagoon insects.
So it is written:
Heal yourself, baby.
With the tree and the touch, with the turmeric.
In this world, nothing brittle prevails,
So in this world, grease is a compliment,
No, it's a weapon,
No, it's a dream you had, where it was cold
And your mother, seeing the threat of gray at your elbows
And knowing that ash is the language of the dead
knelt, and put her hands on your face like this
And anointed you a protected child, a hot iron in a place
of frost.

Recall this, and
Fear no thickness.
Be resurrected, glistening in the story of you.
Be shining.

SIGHT LINES

ARTHUR SZE

I'm walking in sight of the Río Nambé—

salt cedar rises through silt in an irrigation ditch—

the snowpack in the Sangre de Cristos has already dwindled before spring—

at least no fires erupt in the conifers above Los Alamos—

the plutonium waste has been hauled to an underground site—

a man who built plutonium-triggers breeds horses now—

no one could anticipate this distance from Monticello—

Jefferson despised newspapers, but no one thing takes us out of ourselves—

during the Cultural Revolution, a boy saw his mother shot in front of a firing squad—

a woman detonates when a spam text triggers bombs strapped to her body—

when I come to an upright circular steel lid, I step out of the ditch—

I step out of the ditch but step deeper into myself—

I arrive at a space that no longer needs autumn or spring—

I find ginseng where there is no ginseng my talisman of desire—

though you are visiting Paris, you are here at my fingertips—

though I step back into the ditch, no whitening cloud dispels this world's mystery—

the ditch ran before the year of the Louisiana Purchase—

I'm walking on silt, glimpsing horses in the field—

fielding the shapes of our bodies in white sand—

though parallel lines touch in the infinite, the infinite is here—

CLOUD ANTHEM

RICHARD BLANCO

Until we are clouds that tear like bread but
mend like bones. Until we weave each other
like silk sheets shrouding mountains, or bear
gales that shear us. Until we soften our hard
edges, free to become any shape imaginable:
a rose or an angel crafted by the breeze like
papier-mâché or a lion or dragon like marble
chiseled by gusts. Until we scatter ourselves—
pebbles of grey puffs, but then band together
like stringed pearls. Until we learn to listen to
each other, as thunderous as opera or as soft
as a showered lullaby. Until we truly treasure
the sunset, lavish it in mauve, rust, and rose.
Until we have the courage to vanish like sails
into the horizon, or at peace, anchored still.
Until we move without any measure, as vast
as continents or as petite as islands, floating
in an abyss of virtual blue we belong to. Until
we dance tango with the moon and comfort
the jealous stars, falling. Until we care enough
for the earth to bless it as morning fog. Until
we realize we're muddy as puddles, pristine

as lakes not yet clouds. Until we remember
we're born from rivers and dew drops. Until
we are at ease to dissolve as wispy showers,
not always needing to clash like godly yells
of thunder. Until we believe lightning roots
are not our right to the ground. Though we
collude into storms that ravage, we can also
sprinkle ourselves like memories. Until we
tame the riot of our tornadoes, settle down
into a soft drizzle, into a daydream. Though
we may curse with hail, we can absolve with
snowflakes. We can die valiant as rainbows,
and hold light in our lucid bodies like blood.
We can decide to move boundlessly, without
creed or desire. Until we are clouds meshed
within clouds sharing a kingdom with no king,
a city with no walls, a country with no name,
a nation without any borders or claim. Until
we abide as one together in one single sky.

BIOS

Hanif Abdurraqib is a poet, essayist, and cultural critic from Columbus, Ohio. His first poetry collection, *The Crown Ain't Worth Much*, was named a finalist for the Eric Hoffer Book Prize and was nominated for a Hurston-Wright Legacy Award. His collection of essays, *They Can't Kill Us Until They Kill Us*, was named a best book of 2017 by Buzzfeed, *Esquire*, NPR, *Oprah Magazine*, and *Pitchfork*, among others. His most recent book, a *New York Times* bestseller, is *Go Ahead in the Rain*, a biography of A Tribe Called Quest.

Fatimah Asghar is a nationally touring poet, performer, educator, and writer. She is the writer of *Brown Girls*, an Emmy-nominated web series that highlights friendships between women of color. She is a member of Dark Noise and a 2017 Ruth Lilly and Dorothy Sargent Rosenberg Poetry Fellow.

Oliver Baez Bendorf is the author *Advantages of Being Evergreen* (2019), selected for CSU Poetry Center's Open Book Poetry Competition, and *The Spectral Wilderness*, selected by Mark Doty for the Stan & Tom Wick Poetry Prize. His poems have been published in *American Poetry Review, Poetry, BOMB*, and *Troubling the Line: Trans and Genderqueer Poetry and Poetics* and he has received fellowships from CantoMundo, Lambda Literary, Vermont Studio Center, and the Wisconsin Institute for Creative Writing. Born and raised in Iowa, he is currently an assistant professor of poetry at Kalamazoo College in Michigan.

Chase Berggrun is a trans woman poet and the author of *R E D* (Birds, LLC, 2018). Her work has appeared in *Poetry, APR*, the Poem-A-Day series, *jubilat*, and elsewhere. She lives and works in New York City.

Richard Blanco, who was selected by Barack Obama as the fifth Presidential Inaugural Poet in US history, is the award-winning author of two memoirs and four poetry collections. His body of work and advocacy are characterized by his personal negotiation of cultural identity and universal themes of place and belonging. He currently serves as the first-ever education ambassador for the Academy of American Poets and is a member of the Obama Foundation's advisory council.

William Brewer is the author of *I Know Your Kind*, a winner of the 2016 National Poetry Series, as well as the chapbook *Oxyana*, which was awarded the Poetry Society of America Chapbook Fellowship 30 and Under. His poetry has appeared or is forthcoming in *Boston Review, Kenyon Review Online, The Nation*, and *A Public Space*, among others. Formerly a

Stegner Fellow, he is currently a Jones Lecturer at Stanford University. He was born and raised in West Virginia.

Jericho Brown has received fellowships from the Guggenheim Foundation, the Radcliffe Institute for Advanced Study at Harvard, and the National Endowment for the Arts, and he is the winner of a Whiting Award. Brown's first book, *Please* (New Issues, 2008), won the American Book Award. His second book, *The New Testament* (Copper Canyon, 2014), won the Anisfield-Wolf Book Award. His third collection is *The Tradition* (Copper Canyon, 2019). His poems have appeared in *Bennington Review, BuzzFeed, Fence, jubilat, The New Republic, The New York Times, The New Yorker, The Paris Review, TIME*, and several volumes of *The Best American Poetry*. He is an associate professor and the director of the creative writing program at Emory University.

Henri Cole was born in Fukuoka, Japan, in 1956. He has published nine previous collections of poetry and received many awards for his work, including the Jackson Poetry Prize, the Kingsley Tufts Award, the Rome Prize, the Berlin Prize, the Lenore Marshall Poetry Prize, and the Award of Merit Medal in Poetry from the American Academy of Arts and Letters. His most recent book is *Orphic Paris*, a memoir. He teaches at Claremont McKenna College.

Natalie Diaz is the author of *Postcolonial Love Poem* and *When My Brother Was an Aztec*, winner of an American Book Award. She has received many honors, including a MacArthur Fellowship, a USA Fellowship, a Lannan Literary Fellowship, and a Native Arts and Cultures Foundation Artist Fellowship. She is Mojave and an enrolled member of the Gila River Indian Tribe. Diaz is the Maxine and Jonathan Marshall Chair in Modern and Contemporary Poetry at Arizona State University.

Eve L. Ewing is the author of *1919*, the Ironheart series, *Ghosts in the Schoolyard: Racism and School Closings on Chicago's South Side*, and *Electric Arches*. She is a professor at the University of Chicago.

Kathy Fagan is the author of *Sycamore*, a finalist for the Kingsley Tufts Award, as well as four previous collections, including *The Charm*, the National Poetry Series-winning *The Raft*, and Vassar Miller Prize-winner *MOVING & ST RAGE*. Her poems have been widely anthologized and featured in literary magazines such as *The Paris Review, Kenyon Review, FIELD*, and *Poetry*. She has received a National Endowment for the Arts Fellowship, an Ingram Merrill Foundation Fellowship, and served as The Frost Place poet in residence. After graduating with an MFA in poetry from Columbia University, she earned her PhD in English at the University of Utah. She now works as professor of English, director of creative writing, and director of the MFA program at Ohio State University, in addition to serving as poetry editor of OSU Press and advisor to *The Journal*.

Camonghne Felix is a poet, political strategist, media junkie, and cultural worker. She received an MA in arts politics from NYU, an MFA from Bard College, and has received fellowships from Cave Canem, Callaloo, and Poets House. A Pushcart Prize nominee, she is the author of the chapbook *Yolk*, and was listed by Black Youth Project as a "Black Girl From the Future You Should Know."

Louise Glück is the author of more than a dozen books of poems and a collection of essays. Her many awards include the Pulitzer Prize for *The Wild Iris*, the National Book Critics Circle Award for *The Triumph of Achilles*, the Los Angeles Times Book Prize for *Poems: 1962-2012*, the Bollingen Prize, and the Wallace Stevens Award from the Academy of American Poets. She teaches at Yale University and lives in Cambridge, Massachusetts.

Joy Harjo is an internationally renowned performer and writer of the Muscogee Creek Nation and was named United States Poet Laureate in 2019. The author of eight books of poetry and a memoir, *Crazy Brave*, she lives in Tulsa, Oklahoma.

Jane Hirshfield is the author of nine books of poetry, including *Ledger; The Beauty; Come, Thief*; and *Given Sugar, Given Salt*. She is also the author of two now-classic collections of essays, *Nine Gates: Entering the Mind of Poetry* and *Ten Windows: How Great Poems Transform the World*, and has edited and co-translated four books presenting the work of world poets from the past. Her books have received the Poetry Center Book Award, the California Book Award, and the Donald Hall-Jane Kenyon Prize in American Poetry; have been finalists for the National Book Critics Circle Award and England's T.S. Eliot Prize; and have been longlisted for the National Book Award. Hirshfield has received fellowships from the Guggenheim and Rockefeller foundations, the National Endowment for the Arts, and the Academy of American Poets. A resident of Northern California, she is a 2019 elected member of the American Academy of Arts and Sciences and a former chancellor of the Academy of American Poets.

Saeed Jones is the author of *How We Fight for Our Lives: A Memoir* (Simon and Schuster), winner of the 2019 Kirkus Prize for Nonfiction, and *Prelude to Bruise* (Coffee House Press), winner of the 2015 PEN/Joyce Osterweil Award for Poetry and the 2015 Stonewall Book Award/Barbara Gittings Literature Award. The poetry collection was also a finalist for the 2015 National Book Critics Circle Award, as well as awards from Lambda Literary and the Publishing Triangle in 2015. Jones was born in Memphis, Tennessee, and grew up in Lewisville, Texas. He earned a BA at Western Kentucky University and an MFA at Rutgers University-Newark. He lives in Columbus, Ohio.

Fady Joudah has published four collections of poems: *The Earth in the Attic*; *Alight*; *Textu*, a book-long sequence of short poems whose meter is based on cell phone character count; and, most recently, *Footnotes in the Order of Disappearance*. He has translated several collections of poetry from Arabic and is the co-editor and co-founder of the Etel Adnan Poetry Prize. He was a winner of the Yale Series of Younger Poets competition in 2007 and has received a PEN Award, a Banipal/Times Literary Supplement Prize from the UK, the Griffin Poetry Prize, and a Guggenheim Fellowship. He lives in Houston with his wife and kids, where he practices internal medicine.

Ilya Kaminsky was born in the former Soviet Union and is now an American citizen. He is the author of a previous poetry collection, *Dancing in Odessa*, and co-editor of *The Ecco Anthology of International Poetry*. He has received a Whiting Award, a Lannan Literary Fellowship, and a Guggenheim Fellowship, and was named a finalist for the Neustadt International Prize for Literature. His work has been translated into more than twenty languages.

Yusef Komunyakaa's books of poetry include *The Emperor of Water Clocks, Neon Vernacular* (for which he received the Pulitzer Prize), *Talking Dirty to the Gods, Taboo, Warhorses, The Chameleon Couch*, and *Testimony: A Tribute to Charlie Parker*. His plays, performance art, and librettos have been performed internationally and include *Wakonda's Dream, Saturnalia, Testimony*, and *Gilgamesh: A Verse Play*. He teaches at New York University.

Ada Limón is the author of, most recently, *The Carrying*, winner of the National Book Critics Circle Award and finalist for the PEN/Jean Stein Book Award, and *Bright Dead Things*, which was named a finalist for the National Book Award, the National Book Critics Circle Award, and the Kingsley Tufts Award and was named one of the Top Ten Poetry Books of 2015 by the *New York Times*. Her previous collections include *Sharks in the Rivers, Lucky Wreck*, and *This Big Fake World*. She lives in Lexington, Kentucky.

Fred Marchant is the author of five books of poetry, including *Said Not Said, The Looking House*, and *Full Moon Boat*. He is an emeritus professor of English at Suffolk University and lives in Arlington, Massachusetts.

Shane McCrae is the author of several books of poetry: *The Gilded Auction Block; In the Language of My Captor*, which was a finalist for the National Book Award, the Los Angeles Times Book Prize, and the William Carlos Williams Award; *The Animal Too Big to Kill*, winner of the 2014 Lexi Rudnitsky/Editor's Choice Award; *Forgiveness Forgiveness; Blood*; and *Mule*. He is the recipient of a Whiting Award and a National Endowment for the Arts Fellowship. He teaches at Columbia University and lives in New York City.

Hieu Minh Nguyen is a queer Vietnamese American poet and performer and a current Stegner Fellow in Poetry at Stanford University. The recipient of a 2017 National Endowment for the Arts fellowship for poetry, Hieu is a Kundiman fellow, a poetry editor for *Muzzle Magazine*, and an MFA candidate at Warren Wilson College. His work has appeared on *PBS Newshour* and in *POETRY Magazine, Gulf Coast, BuzzFeed, Poetry London, Nashville Review, Indiana Review*, and more. His debut collection of poetry, *This Way to the Sugar* (Write Bloody Publishing, 2014), was named a finalist for both the Lambda Literary Award and the Minnesota Book Award. His acclaimed second collection, *Not Here*, was released by Coffee House Press in 2017.

Sharon Olds was born in San Francisco and educated at Stanford University and Columbia University. The winner of both the Pulitzer Prize and England's T. S. Eliot Prize for her 2012 collection *Stag's Leap*, she is the author of eleven previous books of poetry and the winner of many other honors, including the National Book Critics Circle Award for *The Dead and the Living*. Olds teaches in the graduate creative writing program at New York University and helped to found NYU outreach programs, among them the writing workshop for residents of Goldwater Hospital on Roosevelt Island and for the veterans of the Iraq and Afghanistan wars. She lives in New York City.

José Olivarez is the son of Mexican immigrants. He is a co-host of the podcast *The Poetry Gods*. A winner of fellowships from Poets House, The Bronx Council on The Arts, The Poetry Foundation, and The Conversation Literary Festival, his work has been published in *The BreakBeat Poets* and elsewhere. He is the marketing manager at Young Chicago Authors.

Morgan Parker is the author of *There Are More Beautiful Things Than Beyoncé* and *Other People's Comfort Keeps Me Up At Night*. Her poetry and essays have appeared in *Tin House*, the *Paris Review, The BreakBeat Poets: New American Poetry in the Age of Hip-Hop, Best American Poetry 2016*, the *New York Times*, and *The Nation*. She is the recipient of a 2017 National Endowment for the Arts Literature Fellowship, winner of a 2016 Pushcart Prize, and a Cave Canem graduate fellow.

Carl Phillips teaches at Washington University in St. Louis. His recent books include *Wild Is the Wind* and the prose collection *The Art of Daring: Risk, Restlessness, Imagination.*

D. A. Powell is the author of five collections of poetry, including *Chronic*, winner of the Kingsley Tufts Poetry Award, and *Repast: Tea, Lunch, and Cocktails. Useless Landscape, or A Guide for Boys* received the National Book Critics Circle Award in Poetry. He lives in San Francisco.

Justin Phillip Reed is an American poet and essayist. He is the author of *Indecency* (Coffee House Press), winner of the 2018 National Book Award in Poetry and Lambda Literary Award for Gay Poetry, and a finalist for the 2019 Kate Tufts Discovery Award. He is the 2019–2021 Fellow in Creative Writing at the Center for African American Poetry and Poetics. His work appears in *African American Review, Denver Quarterly, Guernica*, the *New Republic, Obsidian*, and elsewhere. He earned his BA in creative writing at Tusculum College and his MFA in poetry at Washington University in St. Louis. He has received fellowships from the Cave Canem Foundation, the Conversation Literary Festival, and the Regional Arts Commission of St. Louis. He was born and raised in South Carolina.

Ariana Reines is the author of *Mercury* (2011), *The Cow* (2006), and *Coeur de Lion* (2007). Her play *Telephone* was produced at the Cherry Lane Theater and won several Obie awards. Reines was 2009 Roberta C. Holloway Lecturer in Poetry at the University of California Berkeley; she has taught master classes at Pomona College, the University of California Davis, and the University of Pittsburgh. She lives in New York, New York.

Max Ritvo (1990-2016) wrote *Four Reincarnations* in New York and Los Angeles over the course of a long battle with cancer. He was also the author of *The Final Voicemails*, edited and introduced by Louise Glück, and co-authored *Letters from Max* with Sarah Ruhl; both books were published posthumously. His chapbook *Aeons* was chosen by Jean Valentine to receive the Poetry Society of America Chapbook Fellowship in 2014. Ritvo's poetry has appeared in the *New Yorker* and *Poetry*, among many other publications.

Alison C. Rollins, born and raised in St. Louis, currently works as a reference and instruction librarian for the School of the Art Institute of Chicago. She holds a bachelor of science from Howard University and a master of library and information science form the University of Illinois Urbana-Champaign. Rollins has worked for various public libraries, including the DC Public Library and St. Louis Public Library. She is the second prizewinner of the 2016 James H. Nash Poetry contest and a finalist for the 2016 Jeffrey E. Smith Editors' Prize. Her poems have appeared or are forthcoming in *The American Poetry Review, Hayden's Ferry Review, Meridian, Poetry, The Poetry Review, TriQuarterly*, and elsewhere. A Cave Canem and Callaloo Fellow, she is also a 2016 recipient of the Poetry Foundation's Ruth Lilly and Dorothy Sargent Rosenberg Poetry Fellowship.

Rumsha Sajid is a Pakistani-American writer born in Queens, New York. Her work appears in *Halal if You Hear Me* and elsewhere. She lives in Oakland, California, where she works as a housing justice organizer.

Jon Sands is the author of *The New Clean* and the co-host of *The Poetry Gods* podcast. His work has been featured in the *New York Times* and anthologized in *The Best American*

Poetry. He's received residencies and fellowships from the Blue Mountain Center, the Brooklyn Arts Council, the Council of Literary Magazines and Presses, and the Jerome Foundation. He lives in Brooklyn, New York.

Natalie Scenters-Zapico is from the sister cities of El Paso, Texas, USA, and Ciudad Juárez, Chihuahua, México. She is the author of *The Verging Cities* (Center For Literary Publishing, 2015), winner of the PEN/Joyce Osterweil Award, the Great Lakes Colleges Associations New Writers Award, the National Association of Chicana and Chicano Studies Book Award, and the Utah Book Award. She holds fellowships from the Lannan Foundation and CantoMundo, and is a Ruth Lilly and Dorothy Sargent Rosenberg Fellow. She is a professor at Bennington College.

Eleni Sikelianos is the author of six books of poetry, most recently *Make Yourself Happy, The Loving Detail of the Living and the Dead*, and *The California Poem*, which was a Barnes & Noble Best of the Year, as well as hybrid memoirs *The Book of Jon* and *You Animal Machine*. A California native, longtime New Yorker, and world traveler, she now lives in Providence with her husband, novelist Laird Hunt, and their daughter, Eva Grace.

Emily Skaja was born and raised in rural Illinois. She holds an MFA from Purdue University and a PhD from the University of Cincinnati. Her poems have appeared in *Best New Poets, Blackbird, Crazyhorse, FIELD*, and *Gulf Coast*, among other journals. She is the winner of the Gulf Coast Poetry Prize, an AWP Intro Journals Award, and an Academy of American Poets college prize. She lives in Memphis.

Jake Skeets is Black Streak Wood, born for Water's Edge. He is Diné from Vanderwagen, New Mexico. He is the author of *Eyes Bottle Dark with a Mouthful of Flowers*, a National Poetry Series-winning collection of poems. He holds an MFA in poetry from the Institute of American Indian Arts. Skeets is a winner of the 2018 Discovery/*Boston Review* Poetry Contest and has been nominated for a Pushcart Prize. Skeets edits an online publication called *Cloudthroat* and organizes a poetry salon and reading series called Pollentongue, based in the Southwest. He is a member of Saad Bee Hózh: A Diné Writers' Collective and currently teaches at Diné College in Tsaile, Arizona.

Tracy K. Smith is the author of *Wade in the Water; Life on Mars*, winner of the Pulitzer Prize; *Duende*, winner of the James Laughlin Award; and *The Body's Question*, winner of the Cave Canem Poetry Prize. She is also the editor of an anthology, *American Journal: Fifty Poems for Our Time*, and the author of a memoir, *Ordinary Light*, which was a finalist for the National Book Award. From 2017 to 2019, Smith served as Poet Laureate of the United States. She teaches at Princeton University.

Arthur Sze has published ten books of poetry, including *Sight Lines* (2019), which won the National Book Award. His other books include *Compass Rose* (2014), a Pulitzer Prize finalist; *The Ginkgo Light* (2009), selected for the PEN Southwest Book Award and the Mountains and Plains Independent Booksellers Association Book Award; *Quipu* (2005); *The Redshifting Web: Poems 1970–1998*, selected for the Balcones Poetry Prize and the Asian American Literary Award; and *Archipelago* (1995), selected for an American Book Award. He has also published one book of Chinese poetry translations, *The Silk Dragon* (2001), selected for the Western States Book Award, and edited *Chinese Writers on Writing* (2010). Sze is the recipient of many honors, including the Jackson Poetry Prize from Poets & Writers, a Lannan Literary Award, a Lila Wallace-Reader's Digest Writers' Award, a Guggenheim Fellowship, two National Endowment for the Arts fellowships, a Howard Foundation Fellowship, and five grants from the Witter Bynner Foundation for Poetry. His poems have been translated into a dozen languages, including Chinese, Dutch, German, Korean, and Spanish. A fellow of the American Academy of Arts and Sciences, he is a professor emeritus at the Institute of American Indian Arts and was the first poet laureate of Santa Fe, New Mexico, where he lives.

Keith S. Wilson is a game designer, Affrilachian Poet, Cave Canem Fellow, and graduate of the Callaloo Creative Writing Workshop. He is the 2018–2019 *Kenyon Review* Poetry Fellow, and the recipient of scholarships from the Bread Loaf Writers' Conference, the MacDowell Colony, Tin House, Community of Writers, Miami Writers Institute, the UCross Foundation, the Millay Colony for the Arts, and the Vermont Studio Center, among others. Keith serves as assistant poetry editor at *Four Way Review* and digital media editor at *Obsidian*. He lives in Chicago.

Jenny Xie is the author of *Nowhere to Arrive*, recipient of the Drinking Gourd Chapbook Prize, and her poems have appeared in the *American Poetry Review*, the *New Republic, Poetry, Tin House*, and elsewhere. She lives in New York and teaches at New York University. *Eye Level* is her most recent collection.

Kevin Young is the director of the Schomburg Center for Research in Black Culture and poetry editor for *The New Yorker*. He is the author of twelve books of poetry and prose, including the National Book Award-longlisted *Blue Laws: Selected & Uncollected Poems 1995-2015* and *Book of Hours*, winner of the Lenore Marshall Prize from the Academy of American Poets. His collection *Jelly Roll: A Blues* was a finalist for both the National Book Award and the Los Angeles Times Book Prize for Poetry. His nonfiction book, *The Grey Album: On the Blackness of Blackness*, won the Graywolf Press Nonfiction Prize and the PEN Open Book Award, and was a finalist for the National Book Critics Circle Award for criticism. He is the editor of eight other collections and was inducted into the American Academy of Arts and Sciences in 2016.

CREDITS